The Sea Swallow and the Humpback Whale

Written by
Catherine Barr

Illustrated by
Gerry Turley

It is summer in the Arctic, where the sun shines all day and all night.

A polar bear turns his shaggy white head to look up. As he does, an Arctic tern swoops down and strikes the bear's soft black nose with her beak. He ignores her and continues sniffing around for the bird's eggs, which are well hidden on the rocky ground.

The little white tern whirls back up towards the sky. Once summer fades, the tern and her young will take off on an extraordinary journey. But right now, she must keep her eyes on the hungry bear below.

The Arctic tern is one of thousands of 'sea swallows' twisting, turning and diving to protect their nests.

She **strikes** again.

Leaving the tern to fight her battle, a group of explorers step into their kayaks, ready to venture across the icy waters. Hunched up against the cold, they slip quietly out to sea. They are on the lookout for the wildlife of this remote land.

The ragged silhouette of a whale's tail
disappears below the sea's surface. The group
watch in awe at the sight of this magnificent **ocean giant**.

It is a northern humpback whale.
Her 35-tonne body is the size of a bus
and encrusted with lumpy creatures
called barnacles.

It's time for her to feed.

With a slap of her tail, she joins other
humpbacks to scare herring into a circling ball.
The whales dive beneath the fish, before surging
upwards in a feeding frenzy of giant mouths.
They create a curtain of bubbles as they move,
to surround and trap their prey.

The tiny tern dives down to feed on the same fish as the whale. They are about to share the challenge of an epic journey across the globe.

Fuelled by food and guided by instinct,
the whale will swim south towards tropical
waters. There, halfway around the world,
she will give birth to the calf she is carrying.

As a pregnant mother, the whale will be among the
first to leave these rich Arctic feeding grounds.
Followed first by the young and then by the older
whales, she leads a leisurely parade to warmer seas.

The humpback's rippled underwater outline is the last the local people see of her for another summer. She powers out to sea, unaware of the **dangers** lurking in distant waters.

Above her, terns rule the sky. Elegant streaks of white, black and red, the tiny bird and her young are among many, swooping like paper planes tossed into the wind.

As summer days shorten and temperatures drop, even more terns take to the sky. The screeching colony falls eerily quiet, as they circle in their thousands. Known as the 'dread', this strange silence signals that the time has come for the terns to begin their epic voyage.

Over vast expanses of frozen land and deep water, these feather-light birds will fly south in search of seas rich with food.

For months, the journeys of this little bird and giant whale will overlap, as they travel across the North Atlantic Ocean.

Powered by her fast-flapping wings, the tern flies easily on high, strong winds, quickly losing her family in the flock. As she tires, she dips to rest on the waves. But her instinct to find food soon drives her forwards.

Ahead, the humpback surges on. Unlike the bird weaving across the sky, the whale swims in straight lines. For thousands of kilometres, her arrow-like path leads her through the open ocean.

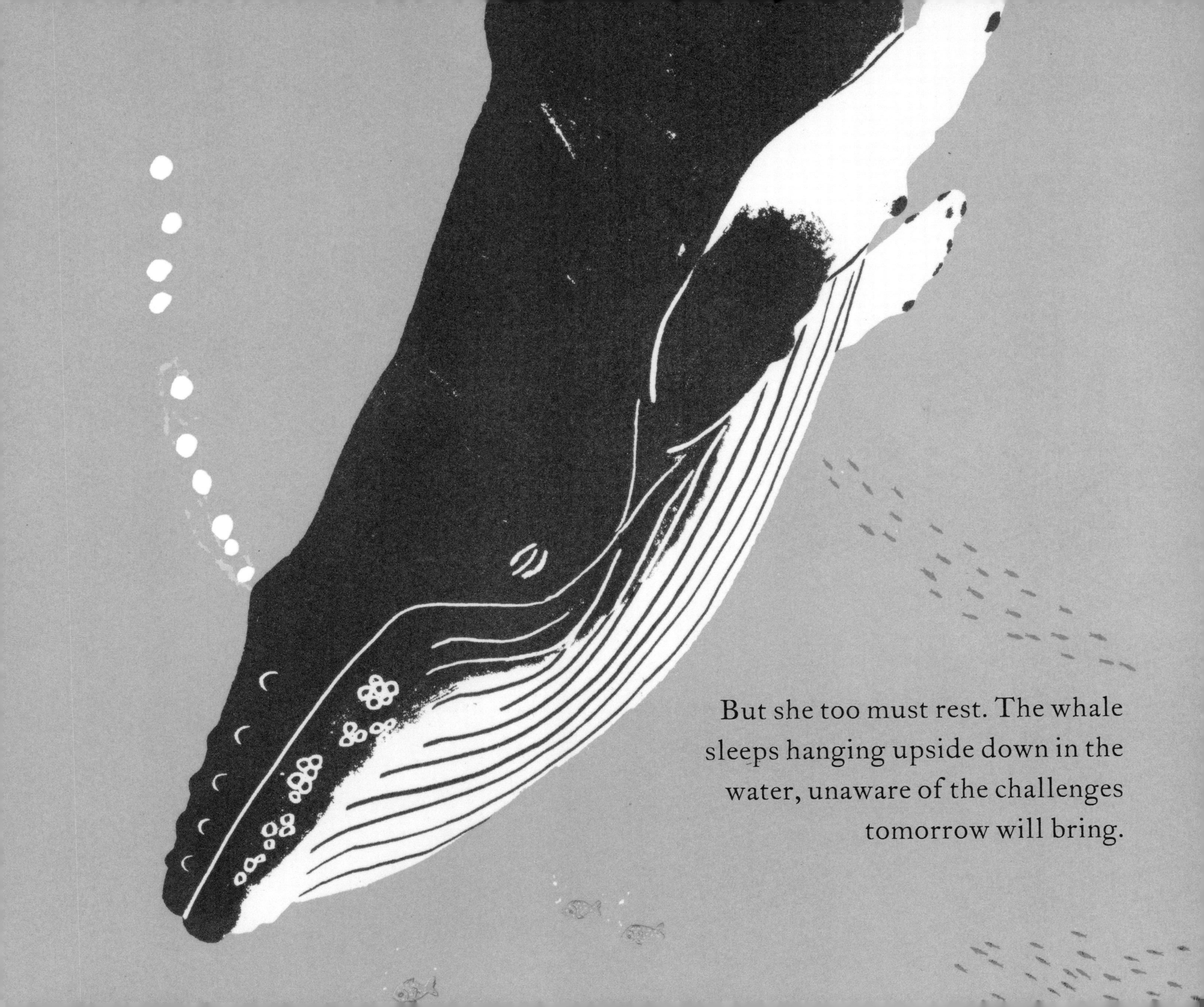

But she too must rest. The whale sleeps hanging upside down in the water, unaware of the challenges tomorrow will bring.

A thundering underwater
echo wakes the humpback,
who plunges forwards
to avoid the unswerving
path of a gigantic ship.

She triples her speed to escape it, but the drifting curtains
of fishing nets confuse her. These **deadly** barriers
threaten her underwater journey.

The ship's captain does not see the whale.
He is watching the rough skies for a storm.
Overhead, the tern is gliding towards dark,
gathering clouds and into trouble.

After weeks of clear skies, the white tips of the waves catch the wind and the skies darken.

On the tern's long journey, she flies with different flocks, soaring between small groups of other migrating terns. They will all reach the southern seas within days of each other.

But now she is quite alone in the gale. Thrown sideways by fierce, icy gusts, the tiny bird struggles to lift herself out of danger. She swoops and sinks in the sky, flying perilously close to the waves.

Lightning **flashes** across her path and the rain pounds her wings relentlessly. Yet the compass in her mind steers her on across the great swell of the ocean.

Eventually, the winds soften and the tern's days become quiet, determined and long. After two tiring weeks, she reaches a place where cold and warmer waters mingle and swirl with fish.

Other birds fill the sky. They keep company with puffins bobbing on the choppy waves.

Over and over again, the tern flies like an arrow up into the sky, before twisting down and plunging into the water to feed. Using their wings as paddles, puffins dart underwater after the same fish.

The tern will feed in this busy, food-rich ocean hotspot for weeks, but in the calm waters far below her, the whale powers on.

Free from the fishing nets and tracing ruler-straight lines once more, her journey continues. After travelling for more than 5,000 km, the humpback finally reaches her destination, halfway around the world.

The rolling moans of the males surround her. The songs of these **singing giants** echo underwater for more than 30 km.

Having completed her long voyage, the whale gives birth to her calf. The pair will rest here for around three months, before returning for another summer at the top of the world.

But **danger** lurks in these turquoise waters. The black fins of killer whales circle the humpback and her newborn calf. Nipping and biting, they try to push the mother away.

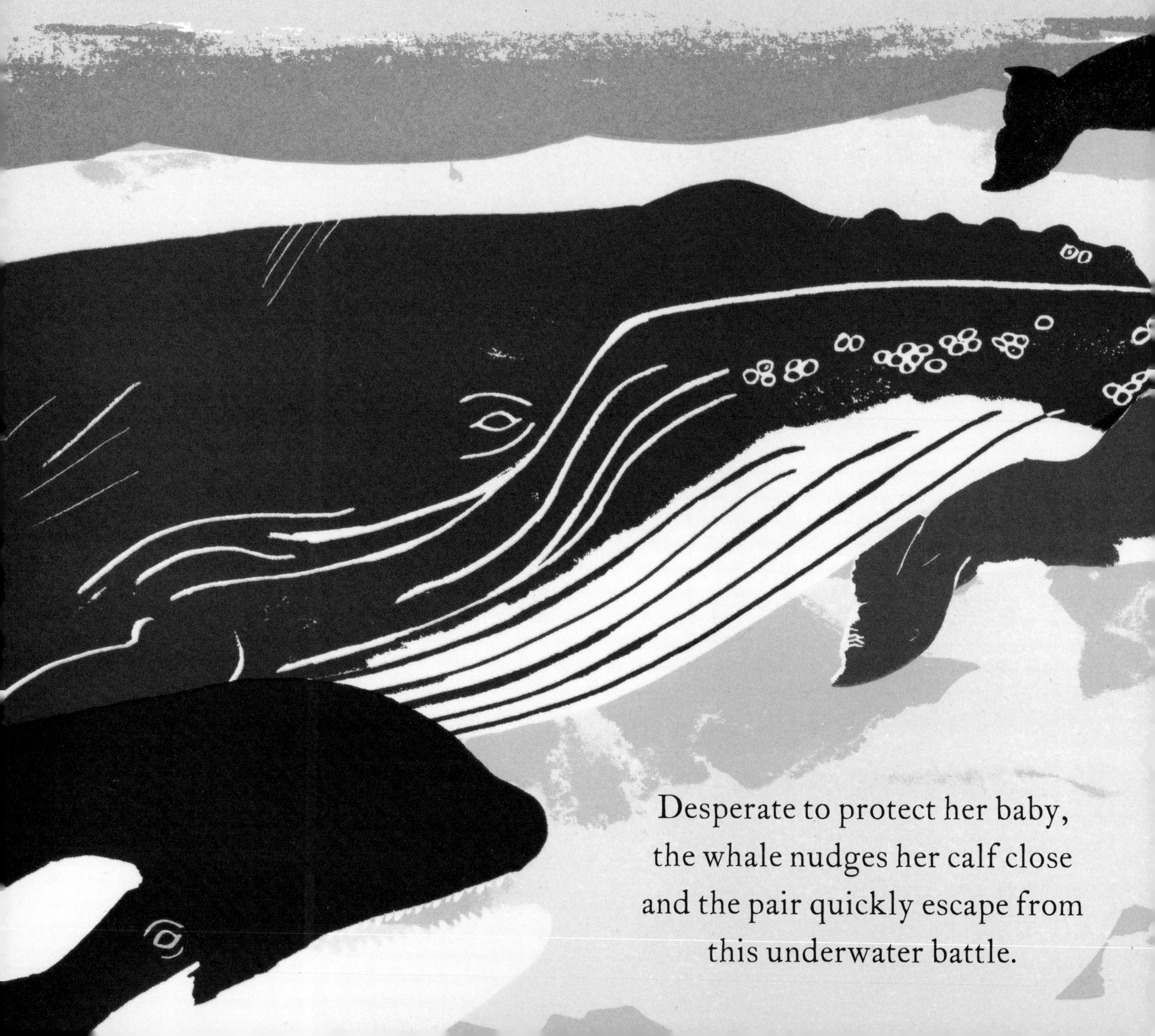

Desperate to protect her baby, the whale nudges her calf close and the pair quickly escape from this underwater battle.

Here, the tern and the whale part. While the whale stays to nurse her calf, the tern flies on, soaring along the sun-drenched African coastline. Her migration traces endless summers, so this 'bird of the sun' sees more daylight in her lifetime than any other creature.

Beyond Africa, she now faces the wildest seas on the planet. Driven by hunger, she strikes out across the giant rolling waves of the Southern Ocean. Harsh winds thrust the little bird into a swirling, screeching mob of hundreds of other terns.

She hovers like a hummingbird, gathered in a feeding frenzy. Below her, the sea is coloured pink with krill – small creatures the size of paperclips that are essential food for most Antarctic life. The krill come together in gigantic swarms, so big they can be seen from space.

The tern **darts** into the icy waters to feed.

At last, the tern has arrived at the southern polar seas. She will stay for the Antarctic summer to feed, gathering energy before her long journey home.

As she makes her way north, she will trace a different path. Instead of long loops and winding tracks, she will fly a simple S-shaped curve up the middle of the South Atlantic Ocean.

After just a few weeks, the litte tern sees the frozen landscape of her Arctic home once more.

The whale is already home. Summer has
returned to the Arctic and its cold, rich
seas are one again teeming with life.

While the whale gorges on herring in the bay, the tern seeks out her mate. They have been apart for months. The two little birds find each other among thousands of Arctic terns and seal their meeting with the delicate offer of a single fish

This is her mate for life. Apart, they have faced extraordinary challenges and they will continue to migrate from pole to pole for another 30 years.

While the whale has travelled over 10,000 km on her journey, it is the tern who breaks all records for animal migrations. Hers is the longest of any creature on Earth – yet she weighs no more than a little bar of soap.

In her lifetime, the Arctic tern will travel the distance of three trips to the Moon and back!

Arctic Ocean

Europe

North America

North Atlantic Ocean

Pacific Ocean

Africa

South America

South Atlantic Ocean

Whale and Tern Migrations

As summer fades, the Arctic tern and the northern humpback whale migrate south. When the humpback reaches the Tropics, she stays to breed, but the tern flies on, gliding down the African coast towards the food-rich southern polar seas. Months later, following the winds north, she joins the whale again in Arctic waters.

Asia

Humpback populations across the world spend summers in icy polar seas and breeding seasons in the tropics. There are northern and southern populations of these whales, but they never meet. As the northern whales head towards the Equator to breed, southern whales head back to the Antarctic to feed.

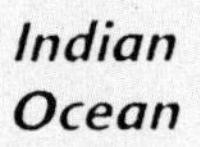

Pacific Ocean

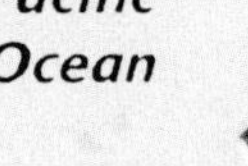

Indian Ocean

Australasia

Southern Ocean

As Arctic terns fly south, they may choose different paths. Reaching tropical waters, some follow the African coastline, while others track the South American coastline in one of the longest known migrations of all animals.

Antarctica

For Lucy, with love. – C.B.

To Helen, Frieda and Iceland. – G.T.

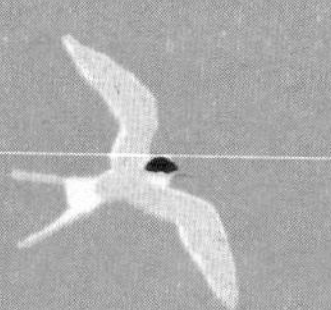

With thanks for expert advice from…

Dr Jen Jackson, British Antarctic Survey

Professor Richard Phillips, British Antarctic Survey

First published in Great Britain in 2021 by Wren & Rook

HB ISBN: 978 1 5263 6081 6
PB ISBN: 978 1 5263 6082 3
E-book ISBN: 978 1 5263 6084 7

10 9 8 7 6 5 4 3 2 1
Wren & Rook
An imprint of
Hachette Children's Group
Part of Hodder & Stoughton
Carmelite House
50 Victoria Embankment
London EC4Y 0DZ

An Hachette UK Company
www.hachette.co.uk
www.hachettechildrens.co.uk

Publishing Director: Debbie Foy
Editors: Phoebe Jascourt and Alice Horrocks
Art Director: Laura Hambleton
Designer: Clare Munday

Printed in China